Be Your Money Hero

5 Steps to Generate the Abundant Life You Were Meant to Live

By Stephani Niblock

Be Your Money Hero - 5 Steps to Generate the Abundant Life You Were Meant To Live

By Stephani Niblock

Copyright © 2022 Stephani Niblock.

All rights reserved. No portion of this book may be reproduced, stored or transmitted in any form except for brief quotations, without prior written permission of the publisher.

Published by Stephani Niblock / Be Your Money Hero

ISBN: 979-8-9866432-0-5 (Print)
ISBN: 979-8-9866432-1-2 (e-book)

Names and personal details of some of the stories in this book may have been changed in order to respect the privacy and personal journeys of those individuals.

This publication is designed to provide accurate and authoritative information in regard to the subject matter covered. It is sold with the understanding that the publisher and author are not engaged in rendering legal, accounting, or mental health advice. If legal advice or other expert assistance is required, the services of a competent professional should be sought out.

To my husband, Joe: You are my champion and my safe place. Thank you for all of the love and support you have given me to help me realize my full potential.

To my kiddos: You are my inspiration. You are heroes and have been entrusted with amazing gifts. You will change the world in awesome ways – the way you have changed mine.

Contents

Chapter One
Take Back Your Life

Chapter Two
Step #1 – Know Thyself...Financially

Chapter Three
Step #2 – Change your thoughts

Chapter Four
Step #3 – Change Your Feelings

Chapter Five
Step #4 – Change Your Words

Chapter Six
Step #5 Change Your Actions

Chapter Seven
Changing Your Habits & Goal Setting

Chapter Eight
Giving, Manifesting
& Making Way for the New

Chapter Nine
Roadblocks Along the Way

⇜One⇝

Take Back Your Life

This was it. After years of struggling to make ends meet, I felt the wave of financial ruin knock the breath out of me.

My 2-year-old daughter came up to me and said that she was hungry in that sweet voice a little girl has. I broke down and curled up in a fetal position in the middle of the living room floor. I had nothing to feed her and her 3-year-old sister except for some frozen peas and a couple eggs left in the refrigerator. Somehow I managed to always keep them fed, but there wasn't enough to go around for me and my spouse.

"I can't do this anymore. I can't survive living like this," I thought, as I convulsively cried into the carpet. "I know that I was meant for so much more than just living day-by-day, paycheck-to-paycheck, not knowing how I am going to keep my kids fed and a roof over their heads. I want…I *need* a life that is peaceful—a life where I don't have to worry about how I am going to survive until my next check comes."

Eighteen months earlier, my spouse and I had filed for bankruptcy. I was working, and he was co-running a bookstore that wasn't making any money. He might have a job here and there, but it wasn't anything substantial. I had become the queen of penny pinching. I could make ten dollars stretch for a week's worth of food for my kids. I was rationing my own food but was surrounded by the most amazing friends and co-workers who would get me lunch a couple times a week. I weighed about 95 pounds and was surviving somehow.

I paid my bills in a very specific order. I knew if my rent check cleared after the other bills, my bank would let me overdraw my account by $499 before they bounced the check. My finances were in ruin so the order things were paid was strategic.

No matter what I did, I couldn't seem to dig out of the hole. My spouse would go to the gas station for a Gatorade and candy bar that was $5 and would rack up $35 in overdraft fees. Things like this happened constantly, and I enabled the behavior by not putting boundaries in place.

Because I wasn't getting the many signs from the Universe that things needed to change, September 26, 2016, gave me signs I could not miss. This was the day I found myself curled up on the floor realizing I could no longer survive in this mess.

I knew in my soul there was more. One of the ways God speaks to me is through numbers and patterns. I kept seeing 333, I knew it was a message of encouragement. I chose to believe that this was a sign I would be okay if I searched for the truth. I chose to tune into gratitude and asked for my guides to send me the strength and wisdom to live the life I knew I was meant to live. When the walls of my life crumbled into ashes, I chose to pick myself up off the floor.

A few days later, the Universe gave me the opportunity to practice boundaries within my relationship. At this time, my spouse and I had an open relationship. My frustration was growing because I saw him finding ways to go see his girlfriend who lived an hour away despite the fact that he didn't have a car. He was able to make things happen for *her,* but refused to stay with our kids while I worked. The next day he told me he was going to San Diego that afternoon.

I felt hurt. I felt betrayed. I'd known him since we were 13 years old. We had been through hell and high water together. I sacrificed everything I had ever known to be with him and had made countless financial sacrifices so that he could do and have the things he wanted. When he told me if I didn't have kids with him he would go find someone else to co-parent with, I caved. Apparently, not even that was enough. He would rather spend his time with another woman who had money and could take him places. The girls and I didn't seem to matter.

That day it became clear to me that despite the love I had for him, I would need to embark alone on a journey to create a better life. I felt hurt and angry. Yet somehow, I also felt free and liberated.

I realized that when we stop trying to control the uncontrollable, when we stop trying to make excuses and take charge of the things we can, the Universe opens the floodgates and gives us all the things we need.

When news of our pending divorce got out, I was overwhelmed with support. My girls' uncles bought them new clothes, and their aunt got us a little car to get us around. Later that month, when I had to move out of the apartment I couldn't afford, my friends lovingly opened their home to me and my daughters.

I knew my girls deserved the best and it was up to me to give that to them. Perhaps I even deserved better as well. And just like that, the journey of a lifetime began.

⤙Two⤚

Step #1 - Know Thyself...Financially

"Whether you want health, wealth, love, freedom, abundance, or anything else in your life, it's not about creating those things; it's about generating them—and then ultimately becoming them."

- Dr. Joe Dispenza

You are about to start learning new things about yourself, and I am excited for you! If you dare to live a better, authentic, full life and are willing to be strong enough to break your current patterns, you can have the life that you were meant for.

You have been conditioned since you were a child with ideas about what you are worthy of, what is possible for you, and what you can achieve. Your experiences have further molded your relationship with yourself, the people around you, and the views you have about the world around you.

You may have been told, "Money doesn't grow on trees," by your grandparents. You may have been taught by watching your parents that rich people are selfish or learned from your peers that when people start making a lot of money they disconnect. Maybe you believe that if you have enough money, you can have whatever you want. And yet, you have become so consumed with your job that you have sacrificed your relationships and what it is that makes you feel alive.

You are meant for so much more than to live paycheck-to-paycheck—to exist in a constant cycle of anxiety. You don't have to be so locked away in your career that you do not have time for yourself, your friends, your family, and to live a great life.

Through this book, you have an opportunity to gain awareness of the subconscious beliefs that are currently sabotaging you and learn strategies for replacing them with truthful beliefs that serve you. You will become clear about what you want from your finances and start taking steps to change your financial reality. You are starting on a journey that will have its share of obstacles, wins, and losses. But you will also be able to come out the other side like the hero you are. You will be tempted to fall back into the known; the old patterns that have become so familiar. But if you hold fast, you will experience the satisfaction of finding your inner truth and breaking those barriers.

Are you ready to start? Let's go!

What Does Abundance Look Like to You?

"Efforts and courage are not enough without purpose and direction."

– John F Kennedy

If you were to take a road trip, you would need to know where you want to go. Otherwise you would just be a wanderer. Intention is necessary to accomplish anything worthwhile, and yet so many people wander aimlessly in their financial lives and end up going around in circles. You are no longer that person. That's why you picked up this book.

You are about to start mapping out what your ideal life looks like and why those things are important to you. Take some time and think about each of these questions and ask yourself why these things are important to you.

What do you want from your finances? (Be specific!)

_____
_____
_____
_____
_____
_____
_____
_____

Why is that what you want? What difference would having those things make? (For example, you might say you want wealth. Why do you want to be wealthy? Would it make you feel safe? Would it impress your dad who said you would never amount to anything? Is it because you would have more influence?)

_____
_____
_____
_____
_____
_____
_____
_____
_____
_____
_____
_____

Who are you as a person in this new life?

_____
_____
_____
_____
_____
_____
_____
_____
_____
_____
_____
_____

Before you start on this next exercise, I want to give you some context. Abundance is more than about just the amount of money you have. It is about the peace, love, and sense of purpose in your life as a whole. I have seen people close to me build successful businesses and wealth at the expense of their time, peace, and relationships.

If you have more money than you can imagine but no real love and peace in your life, is it really worth it? Through this exercise, you will find your "why." It's important to remember why you set out on this path because when decisions and trials come up along your way to abundance, your "why" will help keep you on the right path. Abundance is different for each person, so be specific with what it means to you.

If you could have everything your way, what would abundance look like to you?

_____
_____
_____
_____
_____
_____
_____
_____
_____
_____
_____
_____
_____
_____

What does your life look like when you are living a peaceful, intentional, authentic, abundant life?

_____
_____
_____
_____
_____
_____
_____
_____
_____
_____

What does that life feel like to you?

_____
_____
_____
_____
_____
_____
_____
_____
_____
_____

Congratulations! You just took the first step toward your new bountiful life!

Beliefs

As you begin this amazing adventure, it is important to understand your current relationship to money and how your money stories and beliefs manifest in your life. These could be potential obstacles along the way that need to be addressed.

The beliefs of those around us can shape our own beliefs about money, and those will almost always have to be addressed at some point in our adult lives. Our attitudes and money stories develop over the course of a lifetime. Our childhood experiences can shape our initial views on money and further develop throughout our adult lives. Traumas can also have an effect on our money scripts, triggers, and impulsive behaviors.

I believe these to be the top mental blocks that limit our beliefs about money:

1. <u>You are unworthy.</u>

> *"When you get to a place where you understand that love and belonging, your worthiness, is a birthright and not something you have to earn, anything is possible."*
>
> *– Brene Brown*

I grew up in a conservative Christian household where the standard was perfection. As the boss's daughter and oldest of 12 children, it was my duty to be a prime example for my brothers and sisters, the church, my father's employees, as well as a witness to the lost world around me. I was trained from an early age to be the ideal "helpmeet," accepting that my place in the world was to be a wife and mother. And knowing to step outside what was interpreted as the traditional biblical standard, would mean that I would be ostracized.

When I left the church at 19 years old with my best friend who later became my spouse. I had $13,000 that I used to pay for my first car in cash and get us into an apartment. Not a bad start. However, I struggled not only with feelings of unworthiness, but also with the sense that I was unlovable. I made stupid financial decisions to keep my first husband happy. My sense of not being good enough caused me to be afraid of losing him. I felt it was my responsibility to take care of him and do everything I could to support his dreams. To get him help for his stomach problems, I liquidated my 401(k) to pay for a nutritionist, but he refused to follow her advice. I supported him while he went to college to get a degree in law enforcement. Then I supported him again when he decided to quit school to be a stay-at-home parent. I even supported him while he worked without pay at a bookstore he hoped one day would make money. I continued to support him when he asked for an open relationship. My feelings of unworthiness created an utter lack of boundaries, and that lack of boundaries bled me dry emotionally, mentally, and financially.

As my marriage was drawing to an end, I began to see the truth. There was more than one person in the world who could love me, because I was slowly learning to love myself. Not in a superficial, egotistical way. Rather, I was beginning to see that even if I spent the rest of my days alone, I had value. I was a developing soul, placed on this earth for a reason—as a mother, a friend, and a member of society. I began to find my purpose.

You are on this planet to have experiences that help you evolve and grow spiritually. When you search for truth and love, I promise you, you *will* find it.

You are worthy of love. You are worthy of peace. You are worthy of a financial life that reflects that. As you work through the five steps in this book, you will learn to change your feelings of unworthiness to feelings of self love.

2. Money is evil.

First Timothy 6:10 says, "The love of money is the root of all evil: which while some coveted after, they have erred from the faith, and pierced themselves through with many sorrows."

If you choose to go after as much wealth as you can possibly obtain, regardless of the cost, you will not live in true financial peace. Money after all is an inanimate object. Imagine it as a brick. If you have a big pile of bricks, you can use those bricks to build a home, a hospital, or a shelter for stray dogs. You could also use those bricks to break windows all over town. A brick is neither good nor bad. It is simply a tool you can use to build up, or tear down. Money is no different.

3. <u>Rich people are selfish and greedy.</u>

I once heard that poverty and wealth bring out a person's true character. For example, if you are a generous person, your generosity will change little whether you have next to nothing or more resources than you know what to do with.

If you are a stingy person, you are likely to withhold your resources whether you have a great deal or very little. It's likely you know someone who would give you the shirt off his or her back if you needed it. Do you really believe that person would be any less generous if they had more?

What is important is how you decide to manage your wealth. The more resources you have, the bigger impact you can make. The real question is; what changes will *you* make as you are living an intentional, generous financial life?

4. <u>Making/keeping money is difficult.</u>

We live in an age where access to almost everything is easy, and yet, so many people still believe that making money is difficult. Because of our creative power, we find what we look for.

When you live in chronic stress, this stress causes your imaginative brain to shut down and go into survival mode. You will learn to stop restricting the flow that is within you so that you can awaken that creative flow again. When you are living in a scarcity mindset, you are less likely to take the very actions that could help your financial situation. This may show up such as not asking for a raise, hesitating to apply for that exciting new job, or taking the leap to pursue that million-dollar idea you have.

If you are looking for scarcity, you will find it. If you are looking for opportunity, opportunity is all around you, and you will start to recognize it. If this is a challenge for you, make sure you really dive into the exercises in the Money Scripts section later in this book.

5. <u>You need money to make money.</u>

When I was growing up, my dad would always quote Mr. Miyagi from Karate Kid "Where there is a will, there is a way." There are *many* examples of successful people who started with next to nothing and found their way through the difficulties to reach their dream.

Oprah Winfrey grew up in poverty and experienced abuse. Yet, she was able to secure a scholarship. She had not even graduated when she began her career in media. She struggled with sexual harassment and was even fired, and yet, Oprah continued to show up for herself and built an empire.

The creator of WhatsApp, Jan Koum, grew up in Ukraine and immigrated to the US at the age of 16, where he taught himself computer engineering. By the time Jan was 18, his technological career was taking off. He designed WhatsApp and later sold it to Meta for $19 billion.

Guy Laliberté, the co-founder of Cirque du Soleil, started out as a fire breather who performed on the street. Howard Schultz, the founder of Starbucks, grew up in a low-income housing complex. John Paul DeJoria, who is behind Patron Tequila brand, worked as a kid selling newspapers, ended up in foster care, was briefly in a gang, all before joining the military. Stephen Bisciotti, owner of the Baltimore Ravens, lost his dad at the age of 8 and had to put himself through college.

There is story after story of those who refused to settle with the cards they were dealt in life. Your current circumstances do not determine your future reality.

6. You must make moral sacrifices to have money.

My sister and I held similar false beliefs about money because of what we observed from our parents growing up. I've asked her to share her perspective:

> ### Amber's Story
> *"The main thing that kept me from pursuing wealth was my belief that you have to sacrifice your morals and your family relationships to get and keep wealth. I guess the reason I believed that was because that's what I saw modeled by the only person I knew who made the climb from poverty to wealth-- my dad (also my boss).*
>
> *I saw firsthand how much time it takes to build a business that creates wealth. I saw the mentality that it took, the uninterrupted focus. I heard the lectures and read the books that said you have to be single-minded and relentless in your pursuit of "success." And you must be willing to sacrifice any relationships that distract, discourage, or fail to support you. You must forsake every other part of your life in your pursuit of money. To me, that level of commitment was wrong-- not my definition of success at all. It just wasn't worth it."*

Zig Ziglar and Bob Proctor are two great examples of how you can build wealth by helping others. Zig said "You can have everything in life you want, if you will just help other people get what they want." Bob dedicated his life to helping people tap into the energy of abundance and his legacy continues even though he is no longer on this Earth.

If "wealth" is a word that trips you up, use another word like "abundance" or "prosperity." You get to decide what abundance looks like for you. You may not feel the need to be a billionaire and that is okay. If abundance to you looks like having a homestead with your family living on the land, do that. Abundance is living a healthy, happy, prosperous life. But you do not have to be broke to live in harmony. Financial stress adds to mental, physical, emotional, and relationship stress. When you are worried about money, are you likely to be irritable with your kids or significant other? Do you avoid activities with your friends? Wouldn't you rather live a life in line with your moral values––a life where you can take time off to spend with friends and family without worrying about missing hours at work?

I am a business owner, and I make sure that I spend undistracted time with my family. I block out certain evenings and Sundays on my calendar because these are devoted to family time. I believe I can work hard and still have quality time with my family, nurture the relationships with my husband and children. The way you spend your time and your money should reflect your most important values.

7. <u>More money equals more problems.</u>

    We all have problems, and to be frank, most of them are of our own making. We learn through trial and error, but when we are living our lives, doing the best we can with what we have, every single day––we grow. Having firm boundaries and staying focused on your dream will save you from a world of heartache.

8. <u>You need to hold onto your money.</u>

    If you feel the need to hold onto your money, I'm willing to guess you feel safer when you have money because you've had some bad experiences and perhaps even some traumatic ones. I know this feeling intimately. I know what it's like to have $10 cash to feed your two kids for a week because your bank account is overdrawn. I know what it's like to have your car break when you don't have the money to fix it. This limiting belief to hold on tight to our pennies is intended to protect us, but it is flawed.

    Think of it like this; money has to flow through your life the same way your blood flows through your body. If the blood flow in your body becomes blocked, you can have a stroke. Your body works best when all of the blood is flowing freely, and rhythmically.

    Money is a form of energy, and it also works best when that energy is flowing freely and rhythmically. When you hold tightly to the belief that you do not have enough, two things happen. First, you energetically block abundance from flowing to you. Second, regardless of how much you have, you will never feel you have enough.

Instead, choose to spend, save, and give with intention. (We will talk about this in the coming chapters.) Practice allowing your abundance to flow and create new patterns to bring you peace.

9. I'm just not good with money.

Throughout your life, you may have developed bad habits with money. You have to break those habits by creating new, healthy ones. Habits are choices you make so often that they become natural and automatic. You will have to make new choices over and over again so that those new habits will displace the old. At first, it may feel unnatural, odd, and even scary, but the alternative is to stay where you are forever. We will talk more about habits as well, so keep reading!

10. Money Doesn't Buy Happiness.

Of course money doesn't buy happiness! Being broke doesn't make you happy either. Money does provide options and opportunities. For example, money gives you more therapy options. It gives you the ability to take more vacations, help more people, and make the world a better place. Those things certainly won't make you miserable.

Money Scripts

Brad Klontz identified the following money scripts. You may be pulled toward one or more of these attitudes, and it is helpful to know what your tendency is so that you can keep it in balance.

1. Money avoidance

Money avoidance is when you want to keep money and your financial situation out of sight and out of mind as much as possible.

Mary grew up in a household where her parents were constantly fighting about money. One day, her mom bought her a new dress for Easter and that night her parents got into a raging fight about the money her mother had spent. Because of these experiences, Mary associated money with fighting, anger, and tension. Now she tends to ignore her financial situation as a result. This belief is further confirmed because as she ignores the bills and fails to track her spending, her financial situation is constantly stressful.

2. Money status

Money status is when you correlate the amount of money you have (or don't have) with your value as a person. Self-worth = Net worth.

Jose, is the type of person who would give you the shirt off of his back if you needed it. As a Catholic, he has been taught all his life that the love of money is the root of all evil and that it is easier for a camel to fit through the eye of a needle than for a rich man to enter the kingdom of heaven. Jose associates his lack of money with a higher spiritual self-worth.

My father on the other hand, was the second oldest of 5 children and his mother was practically a child herself. He grew up in poverty in the backwoods of Arkansas on food stamps. He developed an attitude that was a combination of money status and money worship.

3. Money worship

Money worship is where you believe that money can solve all your problems and/or make you feel better. My father grew to believe through his experiences that people who had more money had more control. The formula was simple. If you had enough money, you could fix nearly any problem.

Another example is Sarah. Sarah's father was abusive when she was a child. To "make up" for the abuse, her father would buy her something. As an adult, whenever Sarah has a bad day, goes through a breakup, or is otherwise stressed, she goes on a shopping spree to ease the emotional pain.

4. <u>Money Vigilance</u>

Money vigilance is where you become a penny pincher. You tend to hoard your money. Scrooge is a good example. When you have money vigilance as your script, you may tend to be stingy. If you're like me, you may avoid spending money on new clothes for yourself because you'd rather keep the cash. It can cause friction in your relationships because your significant other sees you as being "cheap."

No script is better or worse than another. Knowing how you generally gravitate can help you recognize when you are out of balance. This provides an opportunity to center yourself and make better financial decisions.

The Human Need for Safety

We as humans have a deep need for safety. The decisions we make with our money can largely be affected by this need. I had coffee with a friend of mine named Alexi Neal. Alexi is a Trauma-Informed Yoga Therapist and Energy Healer at SoulFull Therapy, and the one who brought this truth to light for me.

We find safety in our money in many ways. For me, it is having cash in the bank to fall back on if I need it. For some, it is being able to buy what they want, when they want. For others, they feel safe being accepted by their peers and society and spend money to "keep up with the Jones". It isn't even uncommon for people to feel safe in poverty because they feel that is a requirement for spiritual enlightenment.

We can either ignore our natural tendencies with money, or we can understand and work through them to become better versions of ourselves. If we choose to ignore our relationship with money and sweep it under the rug, we will continue to self-sabotage. Why? Because we are blind to our triggers and natural reactions. But if we choose to become more self-aware, we open the door to personal growth, and develop better habits, narratives, and beliefs about money and abundance.

Exercises

What makes you feel safe financially?

_____
_____
_____
_____
_____
_____
_____
_____

How have your childhood and adult experiences shaped your view of money? Are these views helpful or hindering?

_____
_____
_____
_____
_____
_____
_____
_____
_____
_____

Trauma & Abuse

According to The National Council for Mental Wellbeing, "70 percent of adults in the U.S. have experienced some type of traumatic event at least once in their lives."

There is a spectrum of trauma. It can be one horrible event, constant neglect, or verbal abuse over the course of years. One thing it is not—a contest. Just because it "could have been worse" does not make the effects of your experience disappear. Shoving it down will only cause it to build pressure and eventually explode like a volcano.

Trauma and abuse can affect your beliefs and money scripts, as well as your relationship with money. I grew up in what most people would consider a cult. I was the oldest of 12 children. I was only allowed to wear long dresses and skirts and forbidden to cut my hair. According to my church, a woman's place is "barefoot, pregnant, and in the kitchen." I was not allowed to have a job outside the home—unless it was working for my father (or future husband).

I was taught that because of Eve's transgression thousands of years ago, I would suffer when I had children and periods. I was taught that women are easily deceived and therefore, cannot be trusted to make their own decisions. I was not allowed to ask questions at church. I was told that only my father could answer my questions and questioning his authority or the authority of God would result in punishment and possibly eternal damnation to hell. I was told that a woman is expected to be a subservient "helpmeet" to the man of the house, and it is a wife's responsibility to care for her husband, her children, her home, and her church. She is always expected to put others before herself.

Abuse is swept under the rug. Women are not allowed autonomy or choices, and boundaries are unheard of. If anyone leaves the church, they are believed to be leaving the umbrella of God's protection and the church members are instructed to pray that God will do whatever is necessary to save their soul. (This means the entire congregation is praying that something bad will happen to you to bring you home to the church and save your soul.) When one young man left the church and was in a horrible car accident, it was concluded that God was punishing him for "backsliding."

At 19 years old, I felt dead inside. My best friend and fellow church member confided to me that she was a lesbian. In fear for her soul, I tried to help her reason through her sinful thoughts. But instead, I began to think that maybe she wasn't as wrong as I had been told she was. How could I love someone so completely... how could <u>God</u> love his child so completely and allow her to be damned to hell? How could the church pray for someone to be harmed when the Bible says, "Love thinks no evil?"

In the middle of one cool spring night, I made the scariest decision of my life, took what belongings I could and left. Driving through Denver on I-25 that night was one of the most exhilarating experiences of my life. I felt absolutely free!

It turns out that even when you take the girl out of the cult, the cult retains its grip. The trauma left behind feelings of disconnection, being unlovable and unsafe. I felt shame and a deep sense of unworthiness. I lived in fear that God would punish me for leaving, and my fiancé would abandon me if I couldn't provide enough money to support us. I had no healthy boundaries in any area of my life which drastically affected my finances. For years I allowed my spouse to overspend, remain frequently unemployed, and I overextended myself financially to provide the things he wanted. This was how my trauma led to my financial undoing.

However, trauma and abuse can affect people in many different ways. When it comes to addiction, which is rooted in trauma and used as a temporary escape from reality, it is much easier to see how this sabotages finances. There is the amount of money spent on drugs and alcohol, and the loss of compensation through missed work, and the inability to hold down a stable job.

If you were verbally abused––told you were stupid, worthless, and would never amount to anything––you are far more likely to spend money on people in an effort to be liked and less likely to ask for a raise or look for a better job.

If you were abused by a family member and your abuser bought you gifts afterward as an apology, you may be more likely to go on shopping sprees to cover your emotional pain and discomfort.

What Happened to You by Dr. Bruce Perry is one of the most eye-opening books I have read on trauma. Once you read it, you will never look at humanity the same again. If you are one of the 70 percent of adults who have experienced trauma, you may need to enlist the help of a professional therapist. I believe you will find healing and truth when you search for it and are willing to face your inner demons. I found that as I pursued healing, my financial situation drastically improved. I believe this can happen for you as well.

←Three→

Step #2 - Change your thoughts

"Imagine that your mind is like a garden. You could simply be with it, looking at its weeds and flowers without judging or changing anything. Or, you could pull weeds by decreasing what's negative in your mind. Or, you could grow flowers by increasing the positive in your mind. In essence, you can manage your mind in three primary ways: let be, let go, or let in."

- Rick Hanson "How to Grow the Good in Your Brain"

Your brain develops patterns and neurological networks that grow stronger the more those same patterns are used. It is like creating a path in the woods. If you walk through the woods once, it will not leave much of an impact, but if you take that same path over and over, it becomes worn, evident, and long lasting.

If you have thoughts of scarcity, stress, and worry day after day, this becomes your state of being. In order to change this state to one of gratitude, love, and awe, you have to start consciously filtering your thoughts and create a new neurological pathway. You do this by choosing what thoughts to focus on.

Changing your thought pattern first takes self-awareness. In *The Untethered Soul*, Michael A. Singer talks about our mental voice as "your inner roommate," He explains that you are not your thoughts. You are the being who is aware of those thoughts. Singer goes on to say:

> "Your inner growth is completely dependent upon the realization that the only way to find peace and contentment is to stop thinking about yourself. You're ready to grow when you finally realize that the "I" who is always talking inside will never be content. It always has a problem with something...You think that if you change things outside [of yourself] you'll be okay. But nobody has ever truly become okay by changing things outside. There's always the next problem. The only real solution is to take the seat of witness consciousness and completely change your frame of reference. To attain true inner freedom, you must be able to objectively watch your problems instead of being lost in them. No solution can possibly exist while you're lost in the energy of a problem."

Do you notice that when you're watching a TV show or reading a book that you tend to think about it throughout the day and lose yourself in those thoughts and feelings? What you put into your mind is important because that is what you will dwell on for a time.

When I am dealing with a stressful situation, going through stagnant periods where I feel unmotivated, or world conflict leaves me feeling helpless, I know that I have to put a lot of other good stuff in my mind to keep me from spiraling down a dark path that will take me weeks to recover from. Instead of thinking about conflict and human hurt that I have no control over, I have to make a conscious choice to focus on helping the people that I volunteer for, being a good and present parent to raise good humans, and being the best I can be in my work. I focus on good through meditation, music, reading, and positive relationship connections.

Find what makes you feel empowered, helpful, valuable, and inspired and put your focus on those things to help you create new positive thoughts. When hard stuff comes up in life, know that you are strong and capable of doing hard things. Don't be afraid to ask for help and talk through those hard things with a therapist or a reliable friend.

Your thoughts are the first place that personal change happens because those thoughts become feelings.

Exercises

What thoughts do you regularly have about money?

_____
_____
_____
_____
_____
_____
_____
_____
_____
_____
_____

Where do you think these thoughts and beliefs come from?

_____
_____
_____
_____
_____
_____
_____
_____
_____
_____
_____
_____

⊷Four⇾

Step #3 – Change Your Feelings

"The common meaning of gratitude is to be thankful for benefits received. While this is important, I feel that <u>the energy of gratitude is one of the most powerful attracting forces in the universe.</u>

A heart filled with thanksgiving, even when appearances tell us that we are mired in scarcity, conflict and affliction, moves us to a higher frequency in consciousness and we soon witness reality shining through the illusion."

-John Randolph Price

Take a moment and pick a favorite memory you hold.

Think about those moments. What does it look like?

How did you feel?

What did you taste, smell, see, and hear?

Now observe yourself for a couple of seconds.

Now let's try something else. Think about your favorite pizza—the smell of dough and sauce. See yourself walking into the restaurant as your stomach grumbles with anticipation. Think about the texture of the crust as you sink your teeth into that first bite. Recall how the warm cheese stretches as you pull it away.

Is your mouth watering? Are you suddenly feeling hungry for pizza? When you thought of your favorite memory, did you smile or perhaps even tear up? Why? Nothing changed except for the thoughts you had.

Your mind reacts to your thoughts and turns them into feelings and you can even have a physical response just based on those thoughts. The feelings that you generate with your thoughts carry a lot of energy, and that energy can create physical manifestations that can be used for you or against you.

I consider myself to be naturally pessimistic and skeptical. Ever since I was a kid, my brain goes to the worst-case scenario. I'm like the real-life example of Googling symptoms when you're not feeling well and then thinking your prognosis is certain death. This happens especially when things are good.

For the years following my divorce, I worked tirelessly to rebuild my life. I found and married my best friend. We had a baby and bought a house. Yet, even when everything was going smoothly, life was easy, I found myself tense, waiting for the other shoe to drop. It is easy for me to start down the rabbit hole of feeling fear of loss, scarcity, and unworthiness. So, I have learned a trick.

Have you ever had an annoying song stuck in your head? You finally got rid of it and then it came on the radio or your kids started singing, "We Don't Talk About Bruno" again. What is the best way to get rid of that annoying tune? Change the channel! Put something else on.

We cannot focus on two different things at once and "what you focus on expands" as Oprah says. The same goes for our feelings. We can focus on fear, or love; scarcity or gratitude.

When feelings of stress, doubt, fear, and scarcity arise, change your feelings channel and tune into gratitude and love. Even if you are "naturally negative," training yourself to focus on what you want to attract will become easier and easier with practice.

Your subconscious is a large part of how you react, think, and feel. If you are wired for scarcity, fear, criticism, and worry, you will have to reprogram your subconscious.

If you want to change your programing, change what you are putting into your mind. What music are you listening to? Is it giving you feelings of empowerment and motivation? Is it making you feel free? What are you reading or watching every night? Maybe you are watching the news and now you are struggling with feelings of hopelessness, sadness, and worry? Or you may be reading about ways to improve your skills, learn more about the world around you, or gain useful tools? What conversations are you having? Are they filled with gossip and rumors? Or are your conversations helpful, uplifting, and truthful?

These things may not seem directly related to the feelings you have on a daily basis, but they make a big impact. When you listen to music or a podcast that makes you feel inspired, you are more likely to have a better attitude and better problem-solving skills than if you listen to something like the news channel.

Now don't get me wrong, this is not about ignoring anything that is less than butterflies and rainbows. Of course you must be informed, aware, and prepared for what is going on in the world around you. You must be authentic. I simply ask you to be aware and choose carefully and thoughtfully what you are putting your energy into.

In the world of algorithms, for example, every click you make is being tracked. When you click on a link of celebrity gossip, your algorithm will feed you more celebrity gossip. If you and millions of other people are creating a demand for celebrity gossip, guess what is going to be created? More celebrity gossip.

Your thoughts and feelings work like that as well. The more you focus on something, the more it will come to you. Try this experiment. Think of a blue butterfly. How many have you seen in the last week? Probably none that you noticed. But if you go out this week thinking of blue butterflies, you are likely to see many of them.

For some reason, most people tend to focus on what they don't want, rather than what they do want. Recently, my daughters and I went to the grocery store. We checked out and headed for the car when I realized my keys were not in my pocket. I frantically searched each pocket again to no avail. I quickly jumped to the conclusion that someone had taken the keys from my pocket and stolen my car. We would be stranded and I would have to call my husband and get the police involved. When I checked, however, my car was right where I left it.

I took a deep breath and paused to collect myself. I chased away the negative, frantic thoughts by consciously focusing on feelings of gratitude that the car had not been stolen. We re-traced out steps through the store with no luck and then went to the customer service desk. Waiting in line could be another place where thoughts are likely to start spinning into the "what ifs" but I chose to envision the customer-service lady handing me my keys and how I would sincerely thank her.

When it was our turn, I asked if any keys had been turned in. "Yes," she said and pulled my glorious keys out of the drawer near her. The gratitude I had been feeling as I envisioned her handing me my keys, continued to unfold in real time.

What you focus on expands, so keep your thoughts and feelings pointed at what you want to see in your life.

Another reason to stay focused is that it allows you to keep a clearer mind. In *What Happened to You*, neuroscientist Dr. Bruce Perry talks about how the brain is like an upside triangle. When you start feeling stress, the upper part of your brain—the part that processes logic--begins to shut down. But when you regulate your feelings by taking a deep breath (or several) and choose to envision your ideal turnout, you are better able to reach the steps you need to take to reach that ideal situation.

Take control of your feelings by being aware of what is going into your brain and making wise choices about what you focus your energy on.

Make it a habit to write down and focus on the things you are grateful for each day. Instead of simply writing, "I am thankful for my family." Be specific and write why you are grateful. You might write something like, "I am grateful for my husband because I felt loved and appreciated when he brought me coffee this morning."

Feel free to share these moments of gratitude with those people! You will greatly enhance your relationships and influence others to feel love and gratitude as well.

Exercises

Today I am grateful for_____, because _____:

When I start to feel scarcity, what will I do to change my "feelings channel"?

Five

Step #4 - Change Your Words

> *"Words form the thread on which we string our experiences. Therefore, be careful how you interpret your life. Don't think or speak negatively lest your subconscious and others take you at your word and you are hung by your own tongue!"*
>
> -Aldous Huxley

I took my 7-year-old daughter out with her big sister, and we got a cookie and a bunch of craft stuff to keep her busy on her school break. The day before, she got new shoes and a peppermint hot chocolate from Starbucks. At the dinner table, however, she apparently forgot all that. Her 2-year-old sister got an extra scoop of mashed potatoes (because she refused to eat much else), and my 7-year-old said, "I never get anything!". I looked at her and asked, "Is that the truth you want to speak into existence? Because if that's the case, you can give me back the crafts, and shoes, and I won't bother with treats anymore."

Be careful about what you are speaking into existence. This can be tricky. How many times have you said, "I can't afford that," when you *had* the money in your account, and you just didn't want to spend it on something that wasn't important? Instead of saying, "I can't afford it," upgrade to, "I'm putting that on my wish list!" Rather than saying you are "broke," say you are grateful for that vacation, new outfit, etc. that is coming your way.

Our words can put us in the position of a hero or a victim. When my kids were 2 and 3 years old, I had to go pick up a part for this car that seemed like it was constantly breaking down. I called it the "Cherry Red Hearse '' because that's what it looked like to me, and it was always dying.

After work, I took my girls to the auto part store. They were tired and hungry and so was I. My frustration rose when I realized how much money I would have to spend on my crappy car—and my toddlers were both crying! As we were walking out, I started venting to myself. "I can't make more money because [my husband at the time] won't watch the kids so I can get a second job." When those words came out of my mouth, it was like a lightbulb went off.

I wasn't speaking the truth. I said "I can't" when the truth really was "I won't." I could get a second job. I could grow a pair and tell my spouse that he needed to watch his children; or I could find someone who would be willing to watch them. The truth was I didn't want to rock the boat.

In that moment, I swore to myself that I would always say the truth.

When you use the truthful "I won't" you are no longer the victim. You can't pawn the blame off to someone or something else. Saying "I can't" is easy. If you say "I won't" then you are making a choice and choosing whatever consequence comes with it. It's much better to seriously consider if that is really the choice you want to make. That "I won't" will start becoming a "how do I."

You are writing the story of your life. Use your words wisely so that you write the next chapter you want to live. Speak like the Universe is always listening.... because it is.

Exercises

What phrases do I often use about money?

_____
_____
_____
_____
_____
_____
_____
_____
_____

What could I say instead?

_____
_____
_____
_____
_____
_____
_____

What can I start doing today to improve my relationship with my money?

_____
_____
_____
_____
_____
_____
_____
_____
_____

←Six→

Step #5 Change Your Actions

"Begin with the end in mind."

- Stephen Covey

Once you become intentional with your thoughts, feelings, and words, your actions will begin to shift. Continue to take actions that get you closer to where you want to be. Of course, you need to know where you are, and where you want to be first.

Choose your financial destination. If you are going to take a road trip, you first need to know where you are and where you want to go. From there, you can map out the stops you want to make along the way based on what is important to you. Then find the best route to your destination. Before you start on this road trip, you want to see if there are any roadblocks or if there is bad weather that could impact the route you take. The same goes for your finances.

Take a moment to start mapping out your financial destination. You need a clear understanding of what direction you are going.

Exercises

If you could have everything your way, what would life look like a year from now? Be specific, and describe how you feel in this scenario.

_____
_____
_____
_____
_____
_____
_____
_____
_____
_____

If you could have everything your way, what would life look like in 5 years? How about in 10-20 years? Remember to be specific, and describe how you feel in this scenario.

_____
_____
_____
_____
_____
_____
_____
_____
_____
_____

Why is this the life you want? (Dig deep – until you get to the emotion of it.)

_____
_____
_____
_____
_____
_____
_____
_____
_____
_____

Now that you have a clear picture of what you are working toward, let's jump into action and take an inventory of where you are right now so you can begin to make a roadmap.

Start by taking inventory of your assets as well as your debts/liabilities. You can use the personal balance sheet in this book or you can find budgeting tools at BeYourMoneyHero.com.

Start by listing each of your assets. Assets are things you own that have value, such as your house, car, rental properties, boats, art, jewelry, etc. If you have a loan against the asset, list what is owed along with the interest rate. Then subtract the amount you owe from the net value (see example on the following page).

Next, list your debts along with the interest rates. A debt is anyone you owe money to for any reason. This could be a credit card, payday loan, or that money you borrowed from your friend last year. The net amount will be a negative number. Add up the net amounts, and this will give you your "net worth".

Personal Balance Sheet

Which debt do you want to pay first?
1. Debt with the highest interest rate; or
2. Debt with the lowest balance

As of: __/__/____

Asset / Debt	Interest Rate	Value	Owed	Net
House	5.3	$395,000	$355,000	$40,000
Car	N/A	$15,000	$0	$15,000
Student loan	4.75	$0	$40,000	-$40,000
Credit card	19.25	$0	$4,500	-$4,500
Subtotal:		$410,000	$399,500	
@BeYourMoneyHero			Net Worth:	$10,500

Example

Next, let's talk about the big bad "B" word--BUDGET. I've found there are two types of people when it comes to budgets. You have nerds like me who love them. It's almost like a game. If I set a budget for $500 for groceries for example, I want to see how far I can come under budget. Then I find something else to do with the money that's left over.

For my husband, Joe, on the other hand, "budget" is like a dirty-four-letter word that should not be said in his house. For him, budgets are controlling, and he doesn't want his money telling him what he can and cannot do.

So we are not going to talk about budgets. We are going to talk about spending with intention. I've always thought about money, kind of like taking my little kids to a crowded place. If we were to go to a county fair, for instance, I would tell them before we get there what my expectations are, where they are allowed to go, and what they can do. Otherwise, they would run off to the first shiny thing they see and get lost.

Isn't this what so often happens to our money? Have you ever gotten your tax refund, for example, and ended up spending it on something shiny or it gets spent and you don't know where it went? So instead, what if you become more intentional about how you spend your money?

Dr. Stephen R. Covey tells a story in his book *First Things First* that helps to illustrate how this works. As students fill the classroom, a college professor places a large mason jar on the table. He begins to place rocks about 2" in diameter into the jar until they reach the rim. He turns to the class and asks if the jar is full. The students say "yes".

Next, he pours in pebbles, and they clink around the rocks filling the jar.

The professor then fills the crevices with sand and asks the class again if the jar is full. The class is now a little skeptical but still answers "yes". The professor takes a glass of water sitting on his desk and fills the jar to the brim.

But what would have happened if the professor had attempted to put in the pebbles, water, then sand and then the rocks?

He would not have been able to fit everything into the jar. It would be like getting your check and going out to eat, buying those concert tickets, then paying the bills with whatever you have left and having to eat Raman for the rest of the month.

52

The way we prioritize helps us to make the best use of what we have.

When it comes to spending our money, we are going to use this same philosophy. The rocks represent the things we need in order to survive. These rocks are the <u>basics</u> of:

- Food
- Shelter
- Transportation
- Clothing

The pebbles represent the things that are important to our lives but are not needed for survival. This will be different for everyone but might include things like:

- Insurance (health, life, auto, home etc.)
- Internet
- Child care

The sand represents the things that add comfort and pleasure to our lives such as:

- Entertainment
- Concerts
- Manicures & haircuts
- Going out to eat
- Upgrades to the "rocks" (Food, shelter, clothing & transportation)

The water represents the things we spend money on that are not important to our survival and provide little or no enhancement to our lives. These expenses should likely be completely eliminated.

- Memberships you never use
- Sale items that then sit untouched
- Video streaming services you don't watch
- Credit card interest (eventually)

With this in mind, it's time to start putting together your spending plan. You can find templates at www.BeYourMoneyHero.com. Now spending plans can look quite different, and you will need to find what works best for you and your family. Remember, this is you telling your money where to go. You are in control. You are spending with intention.

You can use a good ol' pen and paper, a spreadsheet, or an app on your phone. (Mint, TrueBill, and YNAB are examples.) Regardless of which method you choose, there are a few key points that should be considered with every spending plan.

1.   This is a learning curve. It will take a few months to figure it out so give yourself some grace in learning this skill.

The first month of using a spending plan you will mostly be tracking your spending to see how it stacks up against how much you <u>thought</u> you were spending. If you are spending less, great! That can easily be adjusted. If you are spending way more than you thought, take a look at that cost and ask yourself if that is an expense you want to keep as is or should you adjust that expense down?

The second month there will be some adjustments but you will see it is becoming a smoother process. By month three, you will have it mostly figured out and may make a few tweaks.

Your spending plan will always be different from month-to-month because your income and expenses may fluctuate. The purpose is that you are spending your money in the way that is authentic to the values you hold such as keeping your family stable, happy, and healthy.

2. Pay yourself and pay it forward first. Make it automatic and keep it out of sight.

Mike Michaelwicz wrote a book called *Profit First* for business owners (a must read if you're self-employed). In it, he says that if you can live on $100, you could likely live on $99 and put that 1 percent aside. Ideally, he suggests putting 10-15 percent toward this "pay yourself first" category, but if you are living paycheck-to-paycheck, you should start off small and grow from there.

For our purposes, we are going to call this PYF (pay yourself first). You take that 1 percent (for example) and put it toward funding for your financial goals.

For starters, you need an emergency fund. Then it will go towards things like debt, retirement, and building wealth, depending on your circumstances. Every situation is different, so talk to a financial professional.

Now for those who are thinking that you could do 10 percent no problem, that's great! Go ahead and put that down on your spending plan sheet and continue on. However, I would offer a word of caution. A spending plan is a tool to help you develop confidence in yourself and your ability to spend wisely. You will build that confidence by making a deposit to your savings and keeping it there until a true emergency should come up. Now, if you put $500 in savings and pull it back out two weeks later because you forgot about a bill, this will only reinforce that voice of doubt in your head. <u>It is okay to start small if you start and build upon that start.</u>

You will be more successful if you make your PYF (pay yourself first) deposits automatic, keeping them out of sight and out of mind. If you have a job that lets you have your check directly deposited into two accounts, start putting that PYF (pay yourself first) money directly into a separate savings account. It's best to use a bank where you do not have your main accounts. This account should be accessible in case you have an emergency, but out of sight so that you are not tempted to use it unless you really need to.

Once you've done that, it's time to take another 1 percent and give intentionally. Again, you can start small, build habits, and grow from there. This is one of the most important and also most difficult steps to take. This is where you stop taking that same neurological path in your brains when it comes to money and start creating a new, abundant path.

Money is energy and energy must flow. If you start feeling fear or scarcity, or feel compelled to tighten your grip on your money, take a deep breath and change your feelings channel to gratitude. I am telling you this as someone who knows what it is like to be dirt broke, you have to start somewhere.

3. Each dollar must have a purpose.

As you are creating your spending plan, every dollar that you anticipate coming in should have an intention for how it will be used. If your income varies, create your spending plan based on what you can reasonably expect to make, and then plan for where the additional income will go as it comes in.

Start with paying yourself and paying it forward first. Then assign the dollars for the "rocks," then the "gravel," and lastly, the "sand." If you have water in your jar, start drying that out and eliminate those expenses as soon as you are able.

Generally, the result should be that all your bills are paid, and you have money left over—money you can use to increase your PYF (pay yourself first) percentage. Take a look over the last few months of bank and credit card statements. Have you forgotten any expenses that are quarterly or annual, such as home insurance, taxes, back to school clothes, etc.? Did you put spending money in your plan? If you are paying all of the bills, you will want to have a little money that you can spend in any (non-destructive) way you want - guilt free!

4. Free up cash flow.

As you are looking at your spending in those first 30 days, consider what may be adjusted. For example, cancel subscriptions that you do not use, review your phone service, take a look at your cable/streaming services. You may want to have your auto and property insurance reviewed, along with your mortgage interest rate and private mortgage insurance (PMI), etc. It pays to make sure those are still a good fit for you.

5. Look at your existing accounts.

If you have retirement accounts, review those as well. If you have old accounts from past employers, you may want to look to see if those funds are being utilized in your best interest. This would be a great time to meet with a financial professional.

⤝Seven⤞

Changing Your Habits & Goal Setting

"A goal without a plan is only a dream."

- Brian Tracy

Now that you are on the path to understanding yourself and making good choices with your money, you need to make this new path "stick." Otherwise, you may find yourself reverting back to your old and familiar ways of doing things.

In the last chapter, I asked you to write down what your ideal financial life looks like. It's time to start breaking that down into bite-size pieces. You can find goal worksheets and resources at BeYourMoneyHero.com.

First, let's look at a snapshot of what a good goal is:

- Yours (and you know why)
- Specific and measurable
- Has a time limit (when applicable)
- Written
- Broken down

Sarah is a single mom of a 5-year-old who wants to "make more money." If she wants this because it's what her *parents* want for her, her efforts will likely fail. This needs to become something Sarah truly wants for herself. It comes down to the "why"—the motivation. Any time you are changing a habit or working toward something worthwhile, you are going to have a hard day, and you may want to quit. What makes you pick yourself up off the floor and dust yourself off is the driving force behind you. So dial into that "why." That's what will help you press through the hard stuff.

Sarah tells me she wants to make more money so she can move, and I ask her why moving is important to her. She says she wants a better house and I ask her "why?" Sarah finally says she wants to make more money because she lives in a rough part of town. Making more money would mean she could move her young son to a safer neighborhood and better school.

Next, what does "make more money" really mean? One extra dollar a year would be more money but is that what you mean? For Sarah, it means making an additional $1,000 a month, and adding $2,000 to her savings for a deposit within 4 months.

Sarah writes down her goal along with her "why" and puts it where she can see it every day. It serves as a reminder, and she thinks about what it will feel like to be in that new home every time her eyes see that paper hanging on her bathroom mirror.

Now that Sarah knows exactly what she wants, she can find ways to bring in that extra $1,000. If she is currently bringing home $15 an hour, she can 1) work an additional 17 hours a week, 2) ask for a raise, 3) make her time more valuable by getting a license, certification, or degree, 4) look at a potential job/career change.

Sarah decided to try several of these options. She asked for a raise, and received a $2 an hour increase in pay. This added $275 to her monthly take-home pay. She is studying for an exam to get a certification within 3 months. This qualifies her for a significant promotion within the company. She also decided to do food deliveries while her son was with her co-parent on the weekends. This would provide money needed for the deposit on a new place. She is now on track to have a new place by her son's birthday.

No goal will be successful unless you stick with it so you have to find how to make goals stick for you. In her book, *The Four Tendencies*, Gretchen Rubin says that people lean toward one of these four categories when it comes to meeting obligations:

- Upholder--Generally meets expectations established by others as well as self-expectations.
- Questioner--Generally meets self-expectations but does not put much weight into expectations set by others

- Obliger––Generally meets expectations established by others but does not follow through with expectations they set for themselves.
- Rebel––Resists expectations and does not like to be committed.

You can take her quiz at quiz.gretchenrubin.com. This will provide you with helpful information about how to work with the way you are wired, change your habits, and reach those goals you set for yourself.

If you lean toward Upholder or Questioner and you are the type of person who sticks to things you believe are important, it would be best to place your goals up where you can see them every day. That way your "why" will propel you to success.

If you are an Obliger and more likely to meet an expectation or goal when someone is holding you accountable, find an accountability buddy. This person needs to be someone you respect; someone who will hold you to the promises you make to yourself.

If you are a Rebel, find an accountability buddy who is willing to impose some type of reward or penalty. For example, if you do not meet your expectations for yourself, you have to make a donation to your *least* favorite political candidate, wear a ridiculous costume in public for a day, or do your friend's laundry for a month. If you are competitive, you could put together a friendly competition with friends or co-workers who also want to work out daily, for instance.

Find out what works for you to stay motivated and accountable. Talking to others who are wired the way you are can give you great ideas too.

←Eight→

Giving, Manifesting & Making Way for the New

"Only by giving are you able to receive more than you already have."

- Jim Rohn

Giving is a necessary part of a happy and abundant financial life. It is part of the flow of financial energy. Religions and cultures around the world speak of the importance of caring for others and sharing what we have. There is something to the sayings "you get what you give" and "you reap what you sow."

Just like spending, giving must be done intentionally. The attitude and feelings behind the giving matters. If you give because you "have to" and feel resentment, I would encourage you to dig deeper into those feelings. Where are those feelings coming from? How can you give out of gratitude for what you have? Start there.

I grew up in a Christian home where a 10 percent tithe was expected and for many this is the ideal amount to give away. However, you may choose to give more or less. If you are just starting, start with 1 percent and increase it over time.

Intentional giving means using your resources wisely. Giving $500 to a well-run charity and giving to a friend who is short on rent (again) do not carry the same value. Giving can become enabling when consistent bad decisions are being made. When choosing where to give, consider the causes that matter most to you. Where can your donation have the most impact? If you're starting at 1 percent or $5 every other week, consider something like buying a bag of dog food for the local animal shelter or a pack of diapers for a family shelter.

You can also donate your time if you find you want to contribute but do not yet have the financial resources. We usually expect volunteering to feel immediately rewarding, but in all honesty it usually just feels inconvenient. However, the impact of helping a teen mom study for the GED, training a puppy at the shelter so it can find a good home, or delivering meals to the elderly are ripples in a pool that can make a great change in the lives of others over time. The way we change the world is by "doing the best we can with what we have now" as Don Miguel Ruiz says in *The Four Agreements*.

I have known caring people who would give someone the shirt off their backs until they had no shirts left to give. This is the other side of being intentional with your giving. In situations where you are pouring more out of your cup than is being poured in, you could end up drowning financially and finding yourself in a position where you cannot help others because you can no longer even help yourself. Giving intentionally includes sticking to your giving boundaries so that you can continue to sustain your impact long-term.

Manifestation

Because our finances are tied into our overall personal growth, it is vital to continue to learn and grow through this process.

Practicing meditation and manifestation can be an important part of this evolution. There may be blocks in your financial journey that seem completely unrelated. Regardless of how busy you are, make your spiritual and personal growth a priority. You can listen to audiobooks while driving or doing laundry, have "No Media Mondays" where your family puts away the phones to read together and talk about what they have learned, or wake up an hour early so that you can have a morning routine that includes journaling and meditation.

In his book *Becoming Supernatural*, Dr. Joe Dispenza speaks about the science behind meditation and manifestation and the importance of bringing yourself into the present moment. He has developed a method for manifestation that I will share today, but I recommend you read his book for a deeper understanding.

Manifestation boils down to two things: create a clear intention and tap into elevated emotions.

- Think of the experience that you want to manifest. What letter or symbol comes to you?
- On a piece of paper, write down the letter or symbol and draw two squiggly circles to represent the electromagnetic field.
- Create a clear intention--Why is this important to you, and what would this manifestation mean for you?
- To the left of the letter or symbol, write the word *"intention"* and specifically list the things you want in this manifestation.
- Think about how you will feel in this new reality.
- Write "Elevated Emotions--the Energy of My Future" on the right side and list those feelings. (Empowered, grateful, safe, love, inspired, etc.)

Bob Proctor taught that we think in pictures. If you have something that you want to generate in your life, create a picture in your mind about what that experience looks and feels like. Picture the person that you are in this experience.

Take time each morning and evening to tap into the elevated emotions. See yourself in the experience you imagine. Lose yourself in that moment, and let the energy surround you.

Through the process of my divorce, I started to write down all the things I was looking for in my future partner. I knew that if I were going to open myself up to marriage again, I needed to be crystal clear about what I was looking for. In this way, I hoped to avoid the hurt and betrayal I felt the first time. I imagined my ideal partner, what energy he had, his characteristics, and how I would feel with him. I'd imagine the life we would build together, and the parent he would be. I even imagined the grandmother that my girls would have because of him and how we would bake cookies together as Christmas music played in the background and giggles filled the kitchen along with the warm smell of sugar cookies. I felt the gratitude, the peace, and the love.

Two years later, I married my husband and my girls were in the kitchen with their Grammy baking cookies and I felt all of the gratitude I knew I would.

The Old Will Fall Away

When you make a commitment to grow, the universe begins to prepare you for your new future.

Most of the time, this means that things that no longer serve you start to fall away. Sometimes those are events that can be perceived as "bad." This might be losing a job or the end of a relationship. The old has to break away to make room for the new.

The universe provides us with experiences that we need in order to grow into the person we are destined to become. When these challenges arise, trust that you will be okay. Feel your way through the loss and grief, and find your way back into love and gratitude.

When I started this journey, I had to start by learning boundaries. When I started putting those boundaries in place, I felt like all the walls of my life crumbled into pieces. I lost my car, my apartment, and my spouse. I had nothing but my kids, my job, and amazing friends. It was one of the hardest, most rewarding things that has happened to me. From the rubble, I rebuilt the life I wanted, and it happened so much faster than I thought it could! I became debt free, found the partner of my dreams, and became a much better parent, friend, and person.

I rose above the survival cycle so that my family and I could thrive. You can do the same.

It's like in any superhero movie—There are dark clouds, the good guys are all beat up in the alley and it seems there is little hope. Then out of nowhere, the hero shows up, and saves the day.

You are the hero in your story.

You are the one who is going to change your whole life for the better. You are writing your story and can write the next chapter. As R.K. Davenport said "Heroes aren't born, they're made." You are transformed into the hero through the pressures that life has dealt by making the choice to get back up and give each day the best you have.

A hero is inside of you at this very moment.

Be Your Money Hero

←Nine→

Roadblocks Along the Way

"Strength doesn't come from what you can do. It comes from overcoming the things you once thought you couldn't."

−Rikki Rogers

It is natural to run into roadblocks in your journey. Those blocks can deter you from moving forward, or they can help you get to know yourself better and become more resilient. You can choose to see those challenges as an opportunity for personal evolution.

Self-Love and Forgiveness vs. Holding On to Resentment

In order for me to fully move towards the life I wanted to live, I had to learn to forgive. I had to forgive myself, my ex, and my father. I had to learn to let go of the resentment. This isn't something you do once and then everything is magically better either. Letting go of the resentment, hurt and bitterness is something that has to be chosen each time you are triggered. It can be a process that you have to work towards.

Forgiveness does *not* mean letting someone walk free, justifying their actions, or implying what they did was okay. Forgiveness means loving yourself enough to refuse to let those toxic feelings continue hurting you; stealing your joy and creativity. Forgiveness is not for the other person, it is for you. It is releasing yourself from their grip. It is one of the biggest (and hardest) ways that you can love yourself.

Guilt and Easing Pain Through Gifts

If you find yourself in the middle of a housing challenge, a death in the family, a divorce, or a number of other hardships; it can be easy to buy things for your child, spouse, or loved one to help ease the guilt you feel or try to ease their pain.

If you are a parent going through a divorce that has been hard on your kids, you may find yourself overextending or excessively buying things for your children in attempts to make amends.

Consider what your love language is. If you feel most loved and cared for when someone gives you a gift, this may be why you feel pulled to give someone else a gift when showing you care. But not everyone is built like this. Your child may feel more love if you spend 15 minutes of uninterrupted time with them, sit quietly working on a puzzle, make their bed, or leave them an encouraging note. If you are trying to comfort your child during a hard time, what a kid usually needs is a listening, present, caring adult to listen to them and help them feel through the hard stuff. A good therapist may also be invaluable help.

If you have a money worship money script like we talked about earlier in this book, you may be using money as a Band-Aid in attempts to cover up or fix a situation when the reality is you do not like the *real* solution. If you are a busy disengaged parent and are throwing gifts at your kids to make up for your lack of presence, you may need to reevaluate how your time is spent. 15 minutes of focused time with your child showing them you care in the way *they* feel most loved, is priceless.

Focusing on the "I can't"

Step #1 is all about becoming aware of your thoughts so that you can start to make new, more helpful thought patterns. If you are focusing on the "I can't", here's how you can start to move past that.

Pull out a sheet of paper if you need to get the negative out of your system and word vomit all over the page. When you are done, get out a new sheet of paper. Start with "if I could have everything my way...." and write what your ideal situation looks like. What would have to be true for that ideal to become a reality. Now, write down "I can move towards this by...." and write down the steps you can take. What are the challenges? Who can help you through those challenges?

When I was in that parking lot with my two toddlers I was having an "I can't" moment. I said "I can't" make more money because my ex wouldn't watch the girls. What I had to do is consider what my ideal solution looked like. I needed to earn a certain amount of extra money by either getting a second job, having a side gig, etc. I could move towards that by either involving the girls in my side gig but that wouldn't be an option if I were to get a waiting job at a restaurant. The challenge was childcare but in speaking with my cousin, he would be able to help watch the girls while I worked.

Perfectionism

Questioners are prone to perfectionism and it can be crippling. (Trust me, I know.) If you are the type that needs everything to be perfect, to know every step along the way, but you get stuck in analysis paralysis, you will need to give yourself a deadline to act. Hold yourself accountable to a third party if needed.

Your spending plan might not be perfect or maybe you don't know which app is best but do not let that stand in your way of taking action. Try out that spreadsheet and make it better along the way but do not get stuck in the details.

Procrastination

If you procrastinate, hold yourself accountable to another person. Set up a reward or consequence for the milestones you set up for yourself. If you need to wear a bright red wig for a day if you fail to meet your expectations but reward yourself for getting the task done, then do it. Work through *The Four Tendencies* to get some ideas for what might work for you.

Being Overwhelmed

When I am overwhelmed, I want to lay down and take a nap. I understand that it can be hard to know where to start when you feel overwhelmed—so much so that you feel you can't move. You can do it! It's okay to ask for help.

If you are underwater financially and do not know where to start, bring in someone you trust to talk through the Actions in Step #5. If you have built up your emergency savings and are overwhelmed or confused about what your next steps are, talk to a financial professional. Start where you can, and you will pick up momentum along the way.

Excuses

"I can't do it differently."

"How my parents did it is the way I've always done it."

"The new way is too hard."

"I'm afraid I can't do it."

You're not afraid that you can't; you're afraid that you *can* and your whole world will change. Change is scary. Change is uncomfortable. You will always have excuses from that "inner roommate" in your head. You have the choice to keep things the way they are, and your circumstances will not change, or you can choose to dive in and take control of your life. You can choose to be the hero of your story and put in the work, or you can choose to settle. It is up to you.

Whenever the excuses bubble up, take a look at your "why". Remember what this hard work will provide for you and your family. Feel the satisfaction you will have when you have pushed through the mud and made for yourself the life you wanted despite the struggles. Picture the person that you are to have made these accomplishments!

Lack of knowledge

My hope is that this book has helped eliminate this road block. The steps in this book will start you on your path to abundance. Additional resources are available at BeYourMoneyHero.com to help you continue your journey.

Conclusion

My daughter has beautiful, long, blonde hair. When she was seven, she always insisted on wearing her hair down, but also happened to be one of the messiest eaters I've ever seen! She would wear a hair tie around her wrist so that when she was eating she could pull her hair back.

One night I made pancakes and she poured warm syrup all over them. She was excited to take her first bite, but her hair was in front of her face and she was about to get it covered in syrup!

"Honey! You are about to make a mess!" I told her just in time to avoid a sticky disaster.

"Your hair tie is on your wrist. It doesn't do you any good if you don't use it."

We have all heard the term, "Knowledge is power." But unused knowledge is just like a hair tie on my daughter's wrist. <u>It doesn't do you any good!</u>

You are an amazing soul. You have been entrusted with skills and gifts from the Universe and have been placed here for a purpose that *only* you can achieve.

You have made it this far, and I believe that you will use this knowledge wisely. I trust that you will continue to learn and grow in abundance.

I look forward to hearing how you have become your money hero and changed your life forever. Share this with me on Facebook, Twitter, or TikTok @BeYourMoneyHero. You can also find more helpful resources, connections and support along your journey at BeYourMoneyHero.com.

Go be your hero and change your world!

← Appendix →

Think of Your Spending Plan Like a Jar

Needed for Survival
- Food
- Shelter
- Clothes
- Transportation

Important
- Insurance
- Internet
- Daycare

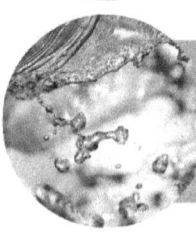

Adds Comfort, Pleasure, or Value
- Upgrades to the "rocks"
- Entertainment
- Going out to eat

Not Important and Little/No Value
- Unused subscriptions
- Buying sale items you never use
- Credit card interest

@BeYourMoneyHero

MONTHLY SPENDING PLAN

Income		Expenses	
Income-1		Month [OR] Pay Period	
Income-2			
Other Income		Pay Yourself & Pay it Forward (PYF)	
Total Income		Minus PYF %	

Rocks (Survival) - Food, Housing, Transportation & Clothes

Bill To Be Paid	Due Date	Amount	Paid	Notes
	Total		Left to Spend	

Gravel (Important) - Childcare, Insurance, Internet, etc.

Bill To Be Paid	Due Date	Amount	Paid	Notes
	Total		Left to Spend	

Sand (Adds Value) - Different for Everyone

Bill To Be Paid	Due Date	Amount	Paid	Notes

@BeYourMoneyHero   Total   Left to Spend

Be Your Money Hero

Bill To Be Paid	Due Date	Amount	Paid	Notes
		Total		

Total Income	Total Expenses	Difference

Notes

@BeYourMoneyHero

Be Your Money Hero

Personal Balance Sheet

Which debt do you want to pay first?   As of: __/__/____
1. Debt with the highest interest rate; or
2.   Debt with the lowest balance

Asset / Debt	Interest Rate	Value	Owed	Net
Subtotal:				

@BeYourMoneyHero   Net Worth:

⊷Acknowledgments⇝

I am so grateful for the outpouring of love and support that has made this book possible! Thank you to my editor, Rebecca Currington, for all of your hard work to turn my manuscript into a work of art!

To my sister and fellow author, Amber Lemus, for helping me find answers to my questions along the way.

To all of my friends and family for cheering me on in my maiden book writing voyage. Thank you!

www.ingramcontent.com/pod-product-compliance
Lightning Source LLC
Chambersburg PA
CBHW032149040426
42449CB00005B/454